CHINA: SHOCKWAVES

CHINA:
SHOCKWAVES

Nancy-Gay Rotstein

Dodd, Mead & Company
New York

No part of this book may be reproduced in any form
without permission in writing from the publisher.
Published by Dodd, Mead & Company, Inc.,
71 Fifth Avenue
New York, N. Y. 10003
Manufactured in the United States of America
Designed by Alice Mauro

First Edition

1 2 3 4 5 6 7 8 9 10

ISBN 0-396-08959-3

Library of Congress Cataloging-in-Publication Data

Rotstein, Nancy-Gay.
China : shockwaves.

1. China—Poetry.   I. Title.
PR9199.3R62C55   1987   811'.54   87-425
ISBN 0-396-08959-3

Frontispiece and part opening illustrations
by **Ma Shiu-Yu**

For Max
With Years of Love

Also by Nancy-Gay Rotstein

Through the Eyes of a Woman
Taking Off

Contents

ACROSS THE EAST CHINA SEA

THE OUTER KINGDOMS

Foreword

Sparse baggage bounced from shiny conveyors of Peking airport.
Returning diplomats, delegations hurried through the small
threshold to be met and swept into waiting gray sedans. My
palms dampened my prized visa, a specially issued permit
allowing me to travel unrestricted within the People's Republic
of China. The customs immigration official, the last Western
reference in which I would luxuriate, replaced search and
seizure with a warm welcome speech and dragged my bags
through the final porthole, permitting me to be instantly met—
by no one. A writer's dream: total freedom elicited—frozen
panic. I was gratefully eyeing the diligence of the mop sweeper,
now the only remaining human figure in the gaping marble
airport. I chose the corner I would hostel for the night or
possibly longer, when an old bandaged survivor appeared. He
gingerly approached me with the indelicate enigma of one not
wishing to confront a problem. Dispassionately, he claimed me,
gathering up the last vestige of Flight #781. Inquiring about
my hotel, I flapped happily through every guidebook I had
stripped from North American shelves.

"Not in book," he said dryly.

"Oh," I jubilated, "it's new!"

"No. Not listed—anywhere."

I was bounced in a springless van for 120 seconds, unceremoniously flopped into The Airport Hotel, a temporary shelter for transient dissidents and foreign oddities. My greeter-chaperone had been placed in the adjacent room.

Next morning, opening my door, I collided with my host. I thanked him for the warm room, aware most hotels are unheated. He flatly assured me that it was not intentional, but the sun's angle. Trying again to bridge the Eastern gap, I thanked him for his concern for my welfare in greeting me outside my chamber. He dourly informed me, with brutal honesty never to reach the definition of local charm, that it was his duty to accompany me to the Peking Bureau. So, without further inflated Western superlatives or outgoing bursts of gushing personality, I quietly demurred into the prearranged car. Once registered, I was granted the unique privilege of individually exploring as a writer, without imposed constraints and from an uninterrupted vantage point, the People's Republic of China.

Today, the micro-visaed visitor is revered, his requests and passage paramount, paradoxically even to the dislocation of the Chinese, and against one's protestations and often acute embarrassment. Never again will immigration and customs be expedited so efficiently as to be nonexistent, mindful, of course, that your sudden appearance on the other side of the hemisphere has long been anticipated.

Transformed overnight from "foreign devil" to honored guest, the visitor is to be learned from, modeled, emulated (but not too closely), courted. Nothing is withheld once official sanction has been granted. This was telescoped for me in one madcap incident reminiscent of Laurel and Hardy.

> Being among two foreigners who were granted passage among a random thousand on the incredible Yangtze River gorges voyage, I was instantly spotted at Wuhan's landing by my zealous woman guide, an emotional replica of Germaine Greer. I was honorably thrust before the slide ramp for instant debarkation. Assertively, she requisitioned passive dock stragglers into reluctant pole-carriers, transformed belligerent vendors into porter nominees, navigated them through people throngs and geese carts, delivering me into a 1950s Russian sedan. From here, we went nonstop through crusted dust streets under instructions for meeting with the comrade-leader. Acute silence greeted my request for the last train departure two hours later to Changsa to connect with the weekly Guilin flight. Balcony tea in swollen armchairs was served with interpreter instruction on Wuhan's industrial achievements. Just when I had relinquished all hopes of the train, the comrade-leader decreed it essential I make the train, now a quarter hour from departure and over a 45-minute car ride removed.

My zealous guide leaped into the car, pulling me behind. A portly man suddenly appeared, imprinting himself into the front seat. With a broad smile from our now comrade-friend, a shout from our guide, we were hurled through Wuhan's rush-hour cobble. Wheels squealed, pedal carts splattered, geese flapped from broken wickers, bicycles collapsed as my revived driver honked enthusiastically. She expounded her newest doctrine. "My comrade-leader has ordered you will have your train." A chaos wake behind, my entourage approached the huge station complex. My rotund friend jumped from the moving car. Seeming to bypass the station, we approached from a rear flank position and suddenly veered onto the platform, launching a four-wheel attack upon incredulous Chinese. I shut my eyes, undecided whether to panic, laugh, or convert for last rites. I opened them to find us tottering by one tire on the platform ledge while still weaving among pylons. The sedan screeched to a stop beside a numbered compartment and gaping Chinese. Our roly-poly friend reappeared, puffing along the track. He pushed me onto the moving train, and with a pitch I felt would instantly qualify him for a pickup football team if he so desired, spiraled my bags, which I now concluded must be elastic, into the opening of the departing diesel.

✻   ✻   ✻

The invited foreigner must not forget that he is entering a world in transition, a paradoxical world flirting with consumerism and private incentives while committed to doctrinaire idealism. The structure is air-suspended on too fragile a guy wire, too rarefied an environment, and with too great a sacrifice for exposure to vulgar adulteration.

The greatest threat to rejuvenated China is ourselves. The North American syndrome asserting privilege and demands is a luxury not permissible here, an acute illness capable of proliferating grotesque dissatisfactions, the malcontent twins of envy and greed. Ultimately, they can undermine relations and speed a return to retrenchment and dark silence.

Nancy-Gay Rotstein
Shanty Bay, Ontario

THE MIDDLE KINGDOM

CHINA TRADER

strangers pulsing through Pacific sky
talking till day became night
to return
talking as silent frames
leap from pin-projectiles,
to dissolve—
talking as suckled infants cry again
into gastric awareness

of grandfather-trader
pampered in foreign concessions
by respect-raped Chinese—
cloistered enclaves, swollen banquets
cloying opulence, gorbelly corruption
aunt dancing into Sun's fading flare

of his own legacied return,
merchant mercenary, dispassioned chronicler
he watched, while oxygen deprived
slashed into Caesarean consciousness
she writhed in bloody afterbirth

FLIGHT COMPANION FROM TOKYO TO PEKING

she shoulder peers into foreign paper
curiosity overruling shyness,
fingers delight in familiar logos
blaze-colors,
she taps, shakes wrapped import package
her bronze-silk face, discovery radiant
her mind, joyous
absorbs the fringes of freedom

FLIGHT #781

a tarmac orphan
jettisoned upon walk machines past vacant runways
unmanned marble counters, spaced elegance—
lone incoming Peking permitees
meticulously visaed, paper expedited
claimed by embassies, cadre legations
in bureaucratic precision
swiftly vanish into preassigned cars
amid Babel chatter's cement echo

myself, misplaced docket
forgotten enigma—panicked
with abundant freedom

IMPASSE

I speed along fresh pavement
masked sweepers massage its dust shoulders
aging figures pedicure shrub
balance debris satchels, waiting human harness

bulldozers crack the good earth's parched crust
a blue uniform constructs
gold-fired geometrics one by one
onto bicycle slab, then pedals away
paced convoy donkey jostles sleeping chaperone

in chunked progression
numbered cement rises opposite
the crumbling mud compounds
interlocking feudal huts
labyrinthed by pitted earth
open on excrement ditch, sewage-wash

stucco horns counterpoint the cyclists' bells
Flying Pigeons transport thrashing ducks
the slashed goat bleeds, billboard stereos bleat
and the master expressway
a gaping cloverleaf impasse
expresses an awakening China

MEMORIAL HALL

they are moved into formation
regimented blue swatches
sectioned across Tiananmen Square
for clocked showing
scrutinized, chatter-restrained by attendant elder;
worker division with dust hats
thick-rimmed middle schoolboys
pigtail classmates,
cotton shoes click on stone rectangles;
demanded hat removal, ordered parting before
solemnity Mao superfigure
imposed upon flowing mountain abstract
the obligated speed walk, side glance
at reposed red-draped founder
stilled in rubberized death

they exit into burnished sunwarmth
cluster-poising workers, hand-touching students
joyous in released animation

GREAT HALL OF THE PEOPLE

alone
in grand auditorium
among padded seats, dialect phones
I face vacuum chairman stage
heaven emblem, flaming flag swords

imported tourist streams
rave of reception filigree
peacock-blossom porcelain
embroidered screen, vibrancy
of Taiwan room's reclaiming mural;
a child-cadre follows
Young Pioneers grip school packs
rooted in awed obedience

in gaping arena, a double alien,
I watch the crimson star radiate
its vortex pulse

TIANANMEN SQUARE

wheels, endless wheels
churning Tiananmen's evening dust mist
resolute faces compress into
swollen blue accordions
blurred cyclists, epoch spinners
press by red-star army child
unafraid with blond stranger
youths touch

across square, unsealed Forbidden City
with ancestral guardians
pressure spokes prod anesthetized dragon
its dry flame tongue flexing

VISIT TO THIRTEENTH MIDDLE SCHOOL

the principal and chief teacher attend
my passage through decayed corridors
whispered lessons gape through ventilation,
window confessors

beneath benevolent father twins, emptied bookshelves
I take my prescribed guest seat

under raw string fluorescents, the instructor extracts
a replay excellence of ideological parsing

a bell rings—programmed eye exercises:
muscles gyrate to cadenced ancestor music,
dismissed into student delight,
girls link fingers, boys hug and laugh

at a silent signal
the eager, animated mass
transforms into an avid corps
perfects drill-squad maneuvers
executes precision war-pack running
with ferocity and enthusiasm

afterward, the robots dissolve again
into smiles, touching, neck embraces
and I am left to ponder
which seedling personality
we will permit to survive

BLOCK CAPTAIN

she rules her numbered cement city
with frozen resolution
she dictates marriage and divorce
living-space rewards

she guides random apartment tour—
music, incense, focal Canadian calendar—
exhibiting her created neighborhood,
the production of women elders
coughing in chill-slab jade workrooms

her commandant face boasts
a slash-smile

FOREIGN CONCESSIONS, 1980s

I sit among Czar alabaster columns
Greek tassel lamps

a room of ambassadors
in Babel clatter

executive reprints,
Wall Street Japanese
tilt rubbed ivory
over vested delicacies,
escrow pocket condiments

micro-chip Koreans
with swollen computer cases
mechanic satchels,
roll polyester sleeves,
their rice bowls suspended

comrade legates relish
privilege abundance,
dangling of coiffured
foreign beauty's
loop gold earrings

shrouded in black cigar Lebanese,
corporate diplomats
meticulous in menu Mandarin
jockey and spin again
in their concentric islands

PEKING GUIDE

between dinner pauses, he lap-glances
the Economist,
gift-reject from leaving British tour
now treasured companion;
when politely possible, he tenders questions
his mind, a fine-tuned counter,
honing knowledge;
he apologizes for inexperience
gifts double hours
fiercely proud of country, heritage

THE AMBASSADOR TO PEKING

alone at Cinderella hour
I enter the emptied enclave;
the ambassador oozes
bourbon and charm
acquired from continental trysts

his wife, a trophy from other postings,
waits in chill museum salon,
porcelain among rare collectibles;
her eyes brighten at gift
of dated journals and texts

he tears at taped pouch,
yearns for news of distant friends
and truth snatches,
mixes lovers, honors, literature
with decanters of Cointreau

the heater sputters
forsakes the frost room
and aging statesman
desperate
in the constraint of China

MING TOMBS

in chill tomb heart
they display canvas sham
didactic mist mockery
pseudo master craft
with mind-fermenting script

the comrades press into airless tube
for their session with Ming abuses,
revengeful peasant contempt;
tyranny graphs, bloated statistics
glare from moist blocks;
they emerge into the clear sunshine
redeemed, contemplative

the angered child
hurls his slingshot
at the privilege limousine
exiting the dust garden
and leaving behind the glazed dragons

THE GREAT WALL OF CHINA

wind twilight
swirls down dragon backside
hurling me into ghosts of wall toilers
bones crushed into debris siding
confronting warring history
soldier colonies, shadow glow
of beacon's tower alarm
echo of carriage horses

spanning desert to sea, undulating protector

here entourage politicians
pose for videos
invade with impunity

flank culture defenses, silently

PERFORMANCE

select guests and wind chill
settle into cement theater with
variety evening respite, pit ensemble accompaniment;
painted hourglass porcelain–
coiffured, scoop gown figurine
with embossed plastic sparkles
announces pantomime comics in tutored staccato,
mannequins swirl daggers
contort muscles to ancestor-prescription,
costumed beauties roller-twist against
snowflake backdrop, suspend from
gyrating bicycle platform to video gasps,
popping of Nikons from second-row management

a vaudeville fantasy
traced among the cabbage mounds

OVERNIGHT IN SHANGHAI

I walk Shanghai's rib
rub bodies, inhale stale breath
of compressed humanity,
crushed in flesh tide

they claim Non Jing Dong
scorn sedan's incessive defense pleas
gape its privileged passengers,
flaunt amplified threats
from sheltered dais police
immobile colonial relics;
disbelievers huddle gyrating Seiko display
motile magician windows
glut vintage movie houses

flash clothes with worker blue
accordion transport among pedicabs
cranes underpinned by bamboo

at dawn
florid track-suited youths
jog past stationary
Tai Ji Quan uniform decade elders

XING GUO GUEST HOUSE, SHANGHAI

*I lie on embroidered crisp sheets
amid carved trunk lacquer
room yawning into room of silken heirloom rugs,
rubbed oak, Empire-splendor chandeliers;
from fat screened veranda, a misted English garden.*

*I remember cursed enclaves
cries of rapier concessions, rabid privilege;
now reinforced metal gate barricades
roadside cabbage decay, factory script boasts,
sheltered legations.*
*Honored envoys again sleep
in transplant Suffolk estate behind walls
cloistered from commitment, Chinese dignity
a neo-colonial apparition.*

ENCOUNTER

wet thuds
from sycamore's aged rubber skin
splatters my Canada pin, bulk parka
a wandering legendeer, dreaming

remnant monster junks
time-snatched huzan processionals
barge relics, black characters
scripted across rust bellies
drift my inner landscape

a mumbled comment
and I am submerged
in an umbrella sea, humanity swells
fluoroscoped, examined with idiom-text English
by probing youths, taboo curious
the fascinated, now brazen
in the obscurity of a swollen hybrid Bund

AS IF THEY HAD NEVER BEEN

they heard of Buddhist
Taoist, Muslims
not Jews
especially not Shanghai Jews
who swelled the scourge-Bund
then fled
with skullcap and silver candles
terror replacing terror

no synagogue or marker
no script character or swatch-allophone
no youth memory

erased
as rice wind

CHINA TIMETABLE

I

Tuesday—at Beijing International

we pass at Beijing airport
company collegians, imported hosts
raise the corporate flag in hype recognition
for arriving sales winners

II

Wednesday—at Shanghai Jing-Jang Club

they reappear with flamboyant salon entrance
demand swan dinner candle and European cuisine
their corpulent bellies engross China problems
of birth control, trade deficit
on stupidity, non-European reasoning

their turgid voices repeat colonial requisites
laud leviathan pool, coolie bowling alley

unheeding students, blundering carbons
of neo-colonial arrogance

HEALTH MINISTRY OFFICIAL

we introduce ourselves
by our national origin
and enouncing his hero's name;
my traveling companion
recalls annual ministry memorial
and boasts a home portrait
in classical posture
of horseback, straw shoes

on parting, he offers advice
on mooncakes and tea-greens
myself, personal heir to Bethune favor

LAKE TAI IMAGES*

mist dragon
with silk wind vapor, sweat phantoms
slips from Louyang to Hanchow
helmed by canal-emperor's will

red-scarfed Pioneers burst into
wood slab barge for reward outing
circling willow nurseries
white bait hatcheries' silvered translucents
webbed oyster harbors;
nesting bamboo shells clog sludge canals;
beside island, fisherman buckets water
into pirate weed camouflage,
draws barren net into flat hull
to mud rhythm from polling barefoot child
woman sprawls boat wash
across tarp sky;
to chuan groan under toil processional
dwarfed by tung oil's black fan
haunting monster specter;
animal peak, ruptured from Tai's stone belly
flares twilight jagged

TWINNED GARDEN CITIES *

coming out of the Wuxi mist,
these weekend globe setters
affirm with poised joviality
their lacquer hair
and spank Ultrasuede,
preening themselves
before hired camera contingent
for next month's council election

* The visit marking the official "twinning" of Wuxi, Jiangsu Province,
and Victoria, British Columbia.

CHUNGKING INCURSION

Asian bone roaches shred
filament grease curtains
in frenzy hunger search
vanishing in black spit pots,
an ancient haunches against
rotting corridor blocks
transported into lotus visions
opium pipe nods fray chin wisps

sidewalk hordes stare, consuming
homosapien curios, rare variety
Marco Polo oddities—
leering faces, eight-deep circle
ensnare in humanity compressor,
squeeze blanched flesh,
ancient swings skewered chicken
another examines caged duck specimen
goose trapped in bamboo basket

sole foreigners on unexpected intrusion
a delicacy import

COMMUNE VISITS

officials greet my scheduled arrival
cloud tea, to rote of commune statistics
private incentives, growth projectiles
precisely interpreter translated;
music path lures to chosen random hut
soft bed, fat pillows, charm resident
and sculpture vegetable beds with mammoth greens,
swirl fish ponds, scrubbed swine pen
Polaroid snap, sugar gum, Yuan expected

an unofficial detour,
I follow smudge wire-hoop host
along patty divide
past oxen, ancient sunk harness deep
among sludge eels
boy scrubbing in mud moss
into seedling courtyard:
barefoot toddlers behind
a pied-piper coterie;
hens dine at bloated potato leaf mounds,
elder squats, scrapes lotus root
inside swine-odor entrance,
sorghum stacks dry against chip-rock frame
garden toiler splatters hoarded human manure
goitered ancient gnaws sweet potato
toddlers cringe from sweets,
hide from instant chronicler

at car's retreat
signal mud boy reappears
skips metal loop down patty path

THE ENTREPRENEUR

collage photos doctored by herbal dyes
promote his recent sideline
as he charms with flowered tie on
curled shirt, zoot suit, fat lapels
brazen from secret storage

his clients ruffle hair
rehearse smiles before polished metal reflector

he centers between
victory arch-span bridge, petal lights
flung above MacArthur's mud-puddle island
Yangtze's interminable flood delta
and throb from crimson factory hills

avoiding the Ancient
satiated by oblivion's rotting dream pipe

EAST IS RED STEAMER

I walk among debris:
masses strewn across tin belly
bodies line plank aisles
a human blanket
routinely scattered for privileged passage
to white cloth diner,
a mother presses baby, shielding
supple frame;
revolutionaries smile from focal gallery
wary uniforms mark my interest
note-taking, feigned poster concentration
docile forms stir, uneasy

I escape below
machine perspiration, body stench merge
haunched basket woman knits
to speaker's eerie chant
of cadenced Jingle Bells
bandaged elder sits immobile
raw pipe drips, spills cold upon his face
youth soldiers joust makeshift checkers
ooze hostile looks

retreat through barrier mattress class
to observing parlor
from squash chairs sleek escape Chinese
returning step cousins
toss cards, munch import biscuits
as wrenched culture roots
unnoticed slide by

GLASS BROTHERS

the aisle sleepers huddle window balustrade
their innocent hands grasp toward display delicacies
child eyes delight in white cloth, ivory napkins
step relatives carve rice wads,
desecrate picture food, sample fish rarities
ignoring glass brothers, hunger whites gleaming
swollen in twilight's cruel refraction

haunted eyes gobble
scarped fish skeleton, egg shreds
the cabbage remnants abandoned on crimson porcelain

compliant, they withdraw to rust corridors
and crusted rice bowls

AMERICAN GEOLOGY PROFESSOR

he hoards his privileged
"soft" cabin and private table
savoring the assigned respect,
shedding visa tie
to farm-scarped nostalgic wife,
children memories, profession commitments,
he pontificates with regal umbrage
gloating over Jurassic rocks, anticlines
to trapped guide-students

third rank academia on Yangtze's current
struggling against obscurity

COMPANIONS

Max and Jurgen
capitalist and communist
executive and East German correspondent
midnight explorers of back streets and Conrad parlors
barter arms linked, Polaroid immortal

fraternal voyage mates
they share confidences, insecurities, laughter

globe barrier debunkers

YANGTZE RIVER GORGES

I

I descend into Dante blackness
sweat bearers, poles harnessed to bone
stagger forms press into rust hull
shrills shriek as thick wash churns the crimson sea

I wake to raging sun:
spindle brush clump on belly hills
slashed falls sprout red syrup
birthing ruffle tiers
of sweet potato and cabbage, hand-sculptured
granite geometrics sheer into Yangtze
above snoozing huo chuan

we strap against Fu Lin's burdened side
hill queues clutter thousand dynasty blocks,
a weaving women processional of
wicker bushels, tubed pepper mustard
carcass rib braces ache across worn plank,
tea vendors barter with deck sleepers
over escape geese cacophony, rooster calls;
behind rails, military maidens flirt
a satchel woman snatches her child's hand

at midnight, we attach to Wan Xian's cliffs:
twinned sisters, placenta tied
share gleaming hunger eye, slash mouth, stench flesh
await dawn's gorge release

II

White King City's fable gateway soars
above sudden swirls that throw me before
scrub mountains, footpath scarred into face
and hatched butcher veins
to release me onto satin wash;
primal peaks tower raw, exposed
as mist echoes enfold

in the distance, Twelve Peak
music canvas tinkles as lime splinters
tool cliff for hive kilns
goat miniatures wander on rock juts
above masked huts, puff swirl betrayed
and heavy toil chant rises
from galley oarsmen as ancient dugout
defies the dark churning current

sky peak dissolves sun
casts beacon light into opaque depths
myself, Tang helmsman
navigating between shroud mountains
foam precipice, whirlpool jettisoned by
shed dragon skin, tossed monster boulders
chill demon fury sears flesh

mountain boys probe for reptile primates
sunset slides across the worn universe

WAN XIAN

belly strapped ferries
beacon lights
lock into mountain stars

I exit through vacuum hold, stench compartment
pig carcass' rot, sweat entrails
swing from rust crusting;
over sprawled aisle claimant
cradling his cackling possession;
up wash tiered steps
into Yangtze's midnight city

path disappears into seamen swollen
rice parlors of steaming vats
dangling pork, skewered duck;
a rooster kill displays
in gutter market
to circle of gnarled faces
delighting in white plumes
bloodstained on cobble;
fruit vendors haggle, tip
yellow pomelo on port-dipped scales;
cacophony of barter clatter, pressed confusion
lure me into fabled narrows

at dawn
pole carriers descend
endless slime stones
a silent processional,
wickers of green mandarins
rattan relay onto snoozing conveyor,
an aged support link
taunting China's ancestral sea

THE GATHERING

they walk through yellow waves
with sickle staffs and wicker bushels
to claim the golden harvest
families slice root with swift base thrusts
deserting thick stubs to soft slog
teams wrist flick, foot crank—
sheaths spit from ancient gobbler
into sheltered refuge, branch discard
swiftly tied, twine-bound
a mother snatches mud toddler
from machine mouth

paddle whine blankets field girls
rising cadence
granny, searching for lost solitary stocks
bends among a tassel sea
reliefed by soaring tabernacle peak

VIEW FROM CATCHING CLOUD PAVILION, GUILIN*

I voyage through caves of dragon teeth
wind chambers protected by stelae and charm poems
to spinning earth table, tied to crystal cloud

below, pulsing China microcosm
a dust city of wicker sweepers, soft sedans
human yolk carts, levered cranes;
farmscape of sludge oxen, straw mud toilers
pedicured communes, nurtured fish hatcheries;
Li River chuan life of
patched tarp families, sweat drag harness
upstream motor launch
disciplined Young Pioneers snatch laughter

a soldier tirelessly scribes praise poems
by Zhu De, Xu Te-li
frocked girls smile, proffer me green mandarins
tenuously

peaks rise from granite crag

LI RIVER CRUISE

visitors stream onto Li River's flotilla
prepared with packaged tables of candies
sliding windows, hot galley service
groups unfurl mandarins as dream magic turns
caves to moon craters, hills to curled lotus petals
as playful dragons, painted horses, bull horns
leap from rock illusion
to dissolve again into granite indifference
sun chatterers stretch topside
pack women sling silken ma bundles
along thirsting bank
others swirl greens from mud plank
steaming chuan village hides,
clusters nuzzle into cave sanctuary
buffalo douse in cool liquid
bow horns locked in mud delight
harness child toils cargo sanpan
across pebble siding
clan hunter releases cormorant spear
as wanderers return for beer chicken banquet
save aged Shanghai teacher, China adoptee
touching each lime shading, life realism
and always those peaks
those tablet peaks, silent

ENGLISH TEACHER
FOREIGN LANGUAGE INSTITUTE, SHANGHAI

we met on Guilin's river journey
her cane thrust at superlatives
in German, English, Chinese
a quarter-century Shanghai teacher
herself a first time tourist
permitted traveler

we meet alone over lunch
Chinese husband absent
conversation starved, unafraid
she speaks of outwitting
interracial love in Fatherland
enduring Mao's confinement
of engineer spouse
she speaks of not belonging
of sand-roots, straining
of recent German pilgrimage
identity search
unexpected alien reaction, self-isolation:
aging history survivor, lost

ESCAPE

I wind-fly, spray pocks porthole
elephant sanpans, mammoth chuan turtles, relic monsters
rise from miscegenetic waters, beyond patrol hunt
before sleek warestore arsenals,
launching commerce pods, dredge silos;
rainbow flashes of dynasty green, empire blue
wash crimson
blur in hovercraft's desperate lunge

HOMECOMING

I cannot adapt to this world
of proffered elegance
of velveteen chairs, bribed kindness, gold toadyism
have I changed
or skin stripped from cataract eyes?

I am haunted by a purpose society
from atrophy and chaos
salvaging intellect
from cold, blistering concrete
restoring pride
from harness paddies, body waste
gifting life
from aged gleaners, dust sweepers
toiling respect
from bamboo and crimson clay
forming dreams

while we, lotus-eaters
consumer mandarins
swirl in monied frenzy
and pleasure analysis

HONG KONG SKYLINE

rigid concrete cubes
geometric reprints
amoeba sprawl, extrude
into compressed mechano skyline,
zip trams, speed ferries, bullet buses
pace traders, shop merchants,
compete elongated hours
robber baron ambitions under Asian smiles

tattered card dwellings
thrown from squatter cliffs
balance on spindle legs in mountain clusters
corrugated soiled decks—stained complements;
Aberdeen junks strain for air shine
salt gnaws engorged bellies
sterns trestle in poverty subdivision
of pork limbs, skeleton fish, torn web nets

an allogenic fusion
of flipped tailpipe
appended to a writhing dragon body

PENINSULA LOBBY

I *watch merchant princes*
swing D'Oyly Carte doors
swashed by miniature sailors
balancing pillbox caps

Asian compatriots sit
at petit four-war table
redefine stratagems
with linguistic fervor
plot market invasion
(finished textiles only)

nanny prims on Viennese brothel seat
beside knickered charges

courting Saks buyer
Australian female designate
mingle season fabric-swatch snippings
with velvet aperitifs and satin glances
beneath laughing plastic masks
and classical flutings

fungus Pakistan reads inert
beside cream pillar

Japanese business clones team
Arab ally-adversaries
demand statistics, instant projections
over lobby clatter, page jangle, dish chatter
assert with ivory smiles and scraping civility
to elicit hypnotic compliance

front desk steward anticipates
lush entrance of poised Asian exquisites,
naval cut-outs again
open polished doors to commerce boudoir

FROM VICTORIA PEAK

I

from Victoria Peak
granite spirals in Pisa illusion
above divided city-harbor,
Kowloon ferry peninsula stretches
toward mythical Asian raft
a retracting, drugged guardian

II

I propel with crowd pace
as fashion employees speed walk,
press shops, restaurants for today's indulgence
in clothes banquets, disco feasts, food swilling
payable in levered salaries, penny stock rolls;
savings purged, their banks recycle money
for Voltaire chess players, continent jockeys;
choreographed ballet cranes swing
with free market rhythm—
built from gold dust, sold for futures

all caught in the cabaret frenzy
of an abbreviated future

ACROSS
THE EAST
CHINA SEA

OSAKA EMBARKATION

jingle chimes soothe attention
                              remote, hypnotic
bamboo click of water vessel
                              in silent landscape
alluring velvet, conditioning
                              emperor citizens
regimenting compliance

company youths, legatees of revered monoliths
mask in Bond cloth, French Cardin
comply with duty-bend:
electropoint leaps placard persuasion

A.B.C. automatons sweep debris
                              in rote will
aluminum porters whisk baggage
                              emit humanity
into computer on-line
                              precision machines
toward tentacled hearth

THE PRICE TAG

metered cabs tick
subliminal sales hype;
nurseries with success ranks
prestige crammers;
restaurant inputs guests
honored visit for rent;
primary competitive entrance
business primers;
dry landscape of peacock moss
shared for coffered piety, fob communion
by austerity monks with worsted habits

efficient computers tally
the cradle suicides

THE OUTING

sheer nylon coordinates
slide along aged tatami, worn cyprus
fawn peacock artistry and rare scroll;
lush brocades with matched crocodile
coquette before gravel sea-garden
of turtle rocks, design moss—
dry austerity landscape of Buddhist earth paradise

with video packs they pan delicacy rooms,
zoom Imperial Abbott's costly aesthetics
quickly edit the Amida Buddha
and token toss at good fortune Ganzah Daishi
to pass hurriedly
to the next ancestor shrine-temple

COUNTRY INN

we desert Tokaido of carts and horn blasts
for dim corridor of screen world
flower urn simplicity and Shinto alcoves

a breeze announces
vegetable and fish delicacies
brought by kimono attendants
who leave us in delicate seclusion

retainers swirl room into lantern memories
soft light casts images
of feudal lords, calligraphers, statesmen
on parchment shades

we, the sole recipients
of fourteenth-generation hospitality
a walled interlude with time

MT. HIEI MONASTERY

up winding monkey freeway they arrive for the day
and bang the warning gong
summoning monks, judiciously absent

soon they head for snacks
from corn hucksters, cake vendors,
student battalions raid
success charms from monk merchants;
the Shinto cow is masoned among
his Buddha captors

sated, they tie fortunes of priest promoters
to burdened snow trees,
and commerce with celibates
beside stark inner chamber;
a lone figure peers
into prayer sanctuary

antic primates observe
money-monk collectors, as the sun
bolts across Saicho's forest retreat

THE FIELD: FOURTH DECADE

they arrive for business served with breakfast
lieutenant with scribe staffman, concealed
in wool and shine polyester, western camouflage,
his English counterpart with rotund wife
snacks eggs and marmalade toast sticks;
disdaining culinary weaponry, they launch oratory
retool opponents' cogent data
disarm request for quantity considerations
dismantle fairness appeal,
silent secretary blitzes logic—
thrusts pre-dawn contracts

mercenaries withdraw, leaving chit unturned
field camouflage untouched
knife beside congealed eggs

THE OUTER KINGDOMS

CAROUSEL

lithe Lippizaners leap
toward storybook stars
exposing golden hoofs,
sleek stallions spring
into frenzied silence,
centaurs carved for
Gepetto-chiseled perfect children
froth frozen foam

music pounds, centrifugal concave
calliope mirrors laughter

golden haired, the lady
sidesaddles gelding
and cradles the enlarged head
of her dreamy, droop-lid son,
fragile frame pressed secure;
his face, glowing,
is haunting in happiness;
her eyes are serene, carefree
as the crystal carousel spins

A SPECIAL SEASON

We walk on coral carpet sand;
air-suspended osprey snatch
squashed child crusts
and surround hand clapping siblings,
satiated wind birds rest
preen salted feathers with beak thrusts;
soft footprints linger on chipped shell-shore

We watch from the tall grass;
ocean mouth froths till air foam
twists down rag-tattered beach
raped of cone-clustered treasures
and covered turtle eggs,
of coon oysters cultivating in
mangrove's tangled thickets;
sea-grape splatters its bittersweet syrup

We fish in wind-soaked mud slicks;
snowy pelicans cling to whipped pine
white dots hinge to evergreen
to plummet, through Christmas chilled sky,
snook and tarpon stalk shallower shelters,
slide into crane canals;
a beached sea trout struggles, strains

We linger beside the brackish lagoon
anhinga arch necks in subaqua snake dance
and spear fish with swift bill-bayonet
surface, shake webbed feet;
roseate spoonbill belly-bobbing on stilts
stir, stalk mud shallows
with fat spatulated clamp;
duckweed webs encircle life's moist roots

We study from torn anthologies
of Caloosa's sand-shell village society,
Ponce de Leon's fatal arrow slash
and fables of female prisoners, pirate brigands;
the chilled sun flamed into eclipse

And we spoke always of the grandmother
gracious, gentle, blessed in memory
who left us with one
silent, shattering heart skip

INNOCENCE

she plops into chill pepper sand
of shell babies and sea fantasies
chatters with beach wanderers
of family, stored dreams;
studies nesting egrets, bellies
dampening in tide cascades,
hears gull whimpers, straw whispers
of wind drying cormorant winged expanse

innocent of the bluefish
who shed the sea in pack hunger,
gnaw baitless lures with razor heat
and the ebb of gular breath
sucked from the white shattered sky giant
to vanish
in night's incessantly black sea-lunge

THE QUESTION

your father's arm cradles questions
of history, heritage torn
from hand-scrawled death diaries,
war journals;
answers, prismed through
forties' black spectacles

your child eyes, luminate
disgorged human cattle cars
Nazi salutes
boy at crossing
holding hand of pince-nez father
unafraid, trusting
both waved to right
in slow procession to barracked death
cadenced to string quartet's
cultured camouflage-passion

I fight the image
blot my eyes
concentrate on soft father-son words
motor whine over silent lake
twilight's silk shadows
Canadian century rooted green:
for you are mine, my son,
my Jewish son,
and I do not know God's future

MOODS *(from a balcony)*

I
Dawn

mist:
a steaming white blanket
pulled over dawn's
sleeping hospice-hills
seals balcony,
aliscaffi whisks into haze;
nestled in nearby alcoves
birds banter bravely,
San Guissippi's spire
soars above cloud camouflaged flagpole,
sailboats disappear

Bisbino's beacon scans
silent sky, searching

II
Noon

a white silk-screened mask,
the heat rises
to trace the virgin hills:
wind lost sailboats stall
in steeping noon sun;
oarsman's face refracts
in stillborn stream;
balcony birds snooze
under sycamore's shade
and the red draped family flag
droops

its century crest
wilting

III
Twilight

suspended above Bisbino hills,
the heat-haze slices
a rainbow ribbon:
hand gliders hover above
Como's twilight currents and soar;
the wind snatches florid sheaths,
wind surfers swerve,
their tottering sails captured;
sailboats bob and tear at tether;
a balcony bird disappears
with twirl dropped
from honeyed croissant delight

Cernobbian church chimes
century-hours, eternal

THE REUNION

you used to sit in
cloistered college room
on oversized Persian pillows
in sleek store jeans
encircled by dream posters
and fat foreign volumes
timbre silken
applauding Shaw and Greer
Schweitzer and Mansfield
boosting Mozart and Mathis
Reverend King and muscled fullbacks

now you sit opposite
a decade removed
behind chocolate almond cake
shawl dumped over marbled shoulders
voice raw
shunning convention deans, major papers
motherhood, marital ties
courting salary politics, chic eateries
motel encounters, lesbian liaisons
censoring memories,
editing potential

we separate at street crossing
paths rent
myself, an unwelcome mirror,
of choices

DECISION

I feel your thoughts
the texture of seasons woven,
stroke birth from fox pups
hurled from earth womb;
hear grain slice black soil
breath sucked through thirsting stocks
gather sequins of rainbow skins
bathed in milk honey,
slide beneath cocoon of latticed lace;
and how to leave plans torn, dreams forgotten
for glistening cathedrals of mind-merchants?
I hear windmusic
and must dance upon crystal suntears

BARGAIN

I dance with demons
upon a jut of stone;
harnessed by furies
to twist in torment
and lured by ledgered taunts
until soul-forsaken, sightless,
I collide with death

THE CHOICE

melancholy spring
seasons, mark a lifetime spent
in pursuit

I choose not the course
but a window
beside bursting ice-puzzles
and tulips,
pungent with birth
to defy the flame figures
that glow and die:
fuel for an ash winter

POWER

they tilt champagne
in padded boardrooms
and toast success,
they pop caviar
and collect for hunger,
at backgammon
they boast of bloodlines
disclaiming prejudice,
they prim for photos
their smiles
knitted by Scandinavian surgeons;
sophisticates of illusion
they have captured our world
and hold us all to ransom

OPTING OUT

I refuse thought,
reject their subconscious birth,
ignore the persistent smack of wasps
licking honey-drops;
blot the imprint of blazing poppies
upon forgotten grave fields.
I suppress all:
yet dreams inject the night,
siphon my sleep
to haunt and confuse

VIENNA VISIT

I stalk cobble-sloped
stained stones
of Judenstrasse,
secured by plaster
walls with chiseled
cherub pediments,
to Stadt Temple's brown
worn wooden doors;
above apartments
across craft shops
synagogue, as decreed,
dissolves into surroundings
sole survivor

gun-carrying polizei
guard square—
pacing, impatient, aloof
police car's pulsing scream
pumps conditioned chilled terror
into charred souls

centuries chanting cadence
of mincha ma'ariv begins

RESEMBLANCE TO ANNE

my darling's eyes
mirror hers
deep and caring,
her coral voice
tumbles the wind,
limbs sprawl among books

but how to forget
the train-children:
skeletons of small bones
emaciated faces
riddled with trust
that stare in shadows of my night?

THE BOND

when we leave this world—
checks, stubs
scrawls of wrenched dreams
for others to patch;
if they love us
they will reach and linger,
then discard
with only a final backward glance
to search for their dreams

EXILE

I saw you pause
air suspended, legs poised
in your Hapsburg hall—
columned gallery, coffered ceiling
Grecian gable plenteous of genei,
with ambassador handmaidens
and princely assistants—
Quadrille Empress led;
watched your perfect figures
cut with precision imposed
by generations of generals
under discipline of nobled masters
executed to Mozart and Strauss

I saw your stallion-leap again
on steamy airless noon of Ontario town
in carnie, acrylic flag-festooned arena
strong of cattle stench
attended by abandoned cottage children
and village transients;
your regal entrance balanced
between plastic-crowned pillars
piaffe scored to squashed
sugar cans' pop, chips' stale crunch
proud lineage seared
into white thigh-flesh
deposed dynasty

LAKE COUNTERPOINT

I

century cedar leaves curl
pale green underbelly raw
birch twigs twist, snap
their sapling stems anguished
hammock tree-belly taut, contorts;
gull and island slab
lunge in convulse wash,
speed creatures dart
for swollen sanctuary,
rain pellets assault earth;
sky-fire crackles

II

seagulls slide across
silvered stream, voices
screech to sky brothers
across bay, boat engine
splices stilled water,
its whine dissolves;
a wind-breath ruffles lake
laps its cool liquid
over ivory stones;
the children's laughter skips
and lingers

COUNTRY FAIR

master unwraps winter fired earth ware
artisan unfolds people-ornaments, Kinsai sequels
others deposit fur rugs, Nizhini Novgorod style
display flesh-wrinkled apple dolls, Stourbridge updates
creators append puppet walkers, batik silks;
booth steam-umbrellas, fuchsia sailcloth
blaze August's color cacophony,
boys pluck bake sale gastronomic legacies
of dowry cupcakes, heritage preserves,
rock minstrels engage locals and cottage carpetbaggers;
parents harness pouch-babies, grasp sugar thumbs of toddlers
children whirl dream kaleidoscopes, circle on sky sweepers
braced grill beef barbecue
wafts across swollen village green

BEACH DAY

toddler crab crawls
onto slick water cot
appended to perfect pedicured toes
then rests dimpled cheeks
on freshly waxed legs
triumphant,
man paces winter-bruised dock
surveys tempest spat glass
diet trunks bulging,
boys, raft-jedis
sprawl slender youth frames
across bobbing star-craft island
gull decorated in
polka-dot wash,
family cat sleeps in
swollen heat
beneath fat August maple
on stuffed cushion
whiskered mouth smiling

AWARENESS

insects pound the night window
pulp their fine fabric
into the frantic search;
a light burns midnight
dark trees
silhouette an awesome scape

and I thrash
with promises not kept
faces I cannot touch;
pain numbs awareness
in my withering frame

a train whistle calls
someplace I shall never go